A Short Catechism
Of the Old Catholic Church

Father Rick Saint, M.Div.

St. Hildegard's Press
Lakeland, Florida

© 2007 Rick Saint

All rights reserved. No part of this publication may be reproduced, stored in a retrieval system, or transmitted in any form or by any means, electronic, mechanical, photocopying, recording, or otherwise, without the prior permission of the copyright owner.

St. Hildegard's Press
PO Box 8966
Lakeland, FL 33806

Printed in the United States of America

ISBN 978-0-6151-4195-4

Introduction

As an Old Catholic priest, seeking to grow a community of believers who were well established in their faith, I found that there is a woeful shortage of good materials published for catechism in the Old Catholic faith. When called upon to teach confirmation classes for new believers, I found myself borrowing from multiple sources, and spending lots of time within the class explaining why Old Catholics don't accept certain beliefs of the Roman Church, the Anglican Church, etc. Out of necessity, I gathered together the resources for this book.

Contained within this resource, you will find all you need to catechize believers in the basics of Old Catholicism. Materials were drawn from a variety of historical documents used by Old Catholics. You will find materials from the Book of Common Prayer, the Utrecht Union of Old Catholic Churches, and other sources generally accepted by all Old Catholic jurisdictions.

At the end of this book, you will find a simple workbook that can be used for confirmation classes. It gives confirmands, as well as anyone who is studying Old Catholicism, a chance to reflect in their own words what we believe.

It is my prayer that you will find this book to be useful to you in your endeavors to grow in your faith and encourage others to do likewise.

                                                            Blessings!
                                                            Fr. Rick

Table of Contents

An Outline of the Faith   Page
1. Human Nature   6
2. God the Father   7
3. The Old Covenant   7
4. The Ten Commandments   8
5. Sin and Redemption   10
6. God the Son   10
7. The New Covenant   12
8. The Creeds   12
9. The Holy Spirit   13
10. The Holy Scriptures   14
11. The Church   15
12. The Ministry   16
13. Prayer and Worship   17
14. The Sacraments   19
    a. Holy Baptism   19
    b. The Holy Eucharist   20
    c. Other Sacramental Rites   21
15. The Christian Hope   22

Appendices
1. The Creeds
    a. The Apostles Creed   23
    b. The Nicene Creed   23
    c. The Athanasian Creed   24
2. The Didache (The Teaching of the Apostles)   28
3. Fourteen Theses of the Old Catholic Church   36
4. Declaration of Utrecht   38
5. A Historic Overview of the Old Catholic Churches   40
6. The Bonn Agreement   45

Catechism Workbook   46

An Outline of the Faith
Commonly called the Catechism

Human Nature

Q. What are we by nature?
A. We are part of God's creation, made in the image of God.

Q. What does it mean to be created in the image of God?
A. It means that we are free to make choices: to love, to create, to reason, and to live in harmony with creation and with God.

Q. Why then do we live apart from God and out of harmony with creation?
A. From the beginning, human beings have misused their freedom and made wrong choices.

Q. Why do we not use our freedom as we should?
A. Because we rebel against God, and we put ourselves in the place of God.

Q, What help is there for us?
A. Our help is in God.

Q. How did God first help us?
A. God first helped us by revealing himself and his will, through nature and history, through many seers and saints, and especially the prophets of Israel.

God the Father

Q. What do we learn about God as creator from the revelation to Israel?
A. We learn that there is one God, the Father Almighty, creator of heaven and earth, of all that is, seen and unseen.

Q. What does this mean?
A. This means that the universe is good, that it is the work of a single loving God who creates, sustains, and directs it.

Q. What does this mean about our place in the universe?
A. It means that the world belongs to its creator; and that we are called to enjoy it and to care for it in accordance with God's purposes.

Q. What does this mean about human life?
A. It means that all people are worthy of respect and honor, because all are created in the image of God, and all can respond to the love of God.

Q. How was this revelation handed down to us?
A. This revelation was handed down to us through a community created by a covenant with God.

The Old Covenant

Q. What is meant by a covenant with God?
A. A covenant is a relationship initiated by God, to which a body of people responds in faith.

Q. What is the Old Covenant?
A. The Old Covenant is the one given by God to the Hebrew people.

Q. What did God promise them?
A. God promised that they would be his people to bring all the nations of the world to him.

Q. What response did God require from the chosen people?
A. God required the chosen people to be faithful; to love justice, to do mercy, and to walk humbly with their God.

Q. Where is this Old Covenant to be found?
A. The covenant with the Hebrew people is to be found in the books which we call the Old Testament.

Q. Where in the Old Testament is God's will for us shown most clearly?
A. God's will for us is shown most clearly in the Ten Commandments.

The Ten Commandments

The Decalogue
1. I am the Lord your God who brought you out of bondage. You shall have no other gods but me.
2. You shall not make for yourself any idol.
3. You shall not invoke with malice the Name of the Lord your God.
4. Remember the Sabbath day and keep it holy.
5. Honor your father and your mother.
6. You shall not commit murder.
7. You shall not commit adultery.
8. You shall not steal.
9. You shall not be a false witness.
10. You shall not covet anything that belongs to your neighbor.

Q. What are the Ten Commandments?
A. The Ten Commandments are the laws give to Moses and the people of Israel.

Q. What do we learn from these commandments?
A. We learn two things: our duty to God, and our duty to our neighbors.

Q. What is our duty to God?
A. Our duty is to believe and trust in God;
1. To love and obey God and to bring others to know him;
2. To put nothing in the place of God;
3. To show God respect in thought, word, and deed;
4. And to set aside regular times for worship, prayer, and the study of God's ways.

Q. What is our duty to our neighbors?
A. Our duty to our neighbors is to love them as ourselves, and to do to other people as we wish them to do to us;
5. To love, honor, and help our parents and family; to honor those in authority, and to meet their just demands;
6. To show respect for the life God has given us; to work and pray for peace; to bear no malice, prejudice, or hatred in our hearts; and to be kind to all the creatures of God;
7. To use our bodily desires as God intended;
8. To be honest and fair in our dealings; to seek justice, freedom, and the necessities of life for all people; and to use our talents and possessions as ones who must answer for them to God;
9. To speak the truth, and not to mislead others by our silence;
10. To resist temptations to envy, greed, and jealousy; to rejoice in other people's gifts and graces; and to do our duty for the love of God, who has called us into fellowship with him.

Q. What is the purpose of the Ten Commandments?
A. The Ten Commandments were given to define our relationship with God and our neighbors.

Q. Since we do not fully obey them, are they useful at all?
A. Since we do not fully obey them, we see more clearly our sin and our need for redemption.

Sin and Redemption

Q. What is sin?
A. Sin is the seeking of our own will instead of the will of God, thus distorting our relationship with God, with other people, and with all creation.

Q. How does sin have power over us?
A. Sin has power over us because we lose our liberty when our relationship with God is distorted.

Q. What is redemption?
A. Redemption is the act of God which sets us free from the power of evil, sin, and death.

Q. How did God prepare us for redemption?
A. God sent the prophets to call us back to himself, to show us our need for redemption, and to announce the coming of the Messiah.

Q. What is meant by the Messiah?
A. The Messiah is one sent by God to free us from the power of sin, so that with the help of God we may live in harmony with God, within ourselves, with our neighbors, and with all creation.

Q. Who do we believe is the Messiah?
A. The Messiah, or Christ, is Jesus of Nazareth, the only Son of God.

God the Son

Q. What do we mean when we say that Jesus is the only Son of God?
A We mean that Jesus is the only perfect image of the Father, and shows us the nature of God.

Q. What is the nature of God revealed in Jesus?
A. God is love.

Q. What do we mean when we say that Jesus was conceived by the power of the Holy Spirit and became incarnate from the Virgin Mary?
A. We mean that by God's own act, his divine Son received our human nature from the Virgin Mary, his mother.

Q. Why did he take our human nature?
A. The divine Son became human, so that in him human beings might be adopted as children of God, and be made heirs of God's kingdom.

Q. What is the great importance of Jesus' suffering and death?
A. By his obedience, even to suffering and death, Jesus made the offering which we could not make; in him we are freed from the power of sin and reconciled to God.

Q. What is the significance of Jesus' resurrection?
A. By his resurrection, Jesus overcame death and opened for us the way of eternal life.

Q. What do we mean when we say that he descended to the dead?
A. We mean that he went to the departed and offered them also the benefits of redemption.

Q. What do we mean when we say that he ascended into heaven and is seated at the right hand of the Father?
A. We mean that Jesus took our human nature into heaven where he now reigns with the Father and intercedes for us.

Q. How can we share in his victory over sin, suffering, and death?
A. We share in his victory when we are baptized into the New Covenant and become living members of Christ.

The New Covenant

Q. What is the New Covenant?
A. The New Covenant is the new relationship with God given by Jesus Christ, the Messiah, to the apostles; and, through them, to all who believe in him.

Q. What did the Messiah promise in the New Covenant?
A. Christ promised to bring us into the kingdom of God and give life in all its fullness.

Q. What response did Christ require?
A. Christ commanded us to believe in him and to keep his commandments.

Q. What are the commandments taught by Christ?
A. Christ taught us the Summary of the Law and gave us the New Commandment.

Q. What is the Summary of the Law?
A. You shall love the Lord your God with all your heart, with all your soul, and with all your mind. This is the first and great commandment. And the second is like it: You shall love your neighbor as yourself.

Q. What is the New Commandment?
A. The New Commandment is that we love one another as Christ loved us.

Q. Where may we find what Christians believe about Christ?
A. What Christians believe about Christ is found in the Scriptures and summed up in the creeds.

The Creeds

Q. What are the creeds?
A. The creeds are statements of our basic beliefs about God.

Q. How many creeds does this Church use in its worship?
A. This Church uses two creeds: The Apostles' Creed and the Nicene Creed.

Q. What is the Apostles' Creed?
A. The Apostles' Creed is the ancient creed of Baptism; it is used in the Church's daily worship to recall our Baptismal Covenant.

Q. What is the Nicene Creed?
A. The Nicene Creed is the creed of the universal Church and is used at the Eucharist.

Q. What, then, is the Athanasian Creed?
A. The Athanasian Creed is an ancient document proclaiming the nature of the Incarnation and of God as Trinity.

Q. What is the Trinity?
A. The Trinity is one God: Father, Son, and Holy Spirit.

The Holy Spirit

Q. What is the Holy Spirit?
A. The Holy Spirit is the Third Person of the Trinity, God at work in the world and in the Church even now.

Q. How is the Holy Spirit revealed in the Old Covenant?
A. The Holy Spirit is revealed in the Old Covenant as the giver of life, the One who spoke through the prophets.

Q. How is the Holy Spirit revealed in the New Covenant?
A. The Holy Spirit is revealed as the Lord who leads us into all truth and enables us to grow in the likeness of Christ.

Q. How do we recognize the presence of the Holy Spirit in our lives?
A. We recognize the presence of the Holy Spirit when we confess Jesus Christ as Lord and are brought into love and harmony with God, with ourselves, with our neighbors, and with all creation.

Q. How do we recognize the truths taught by the Holy Spirit?
A. We recognize truths to be taught by the Holy Spirit when they are in accord with the Scriptures.

The Holy Scriptures

Q. What are the Holy Scriptures?
A. The Holy Scriptures, commonly called the Bible, are the books of the Old and New Testaments; other books, called the Apocrypha, are often included in the Bible.

Q. What is the Old Testament?
A. The Old Testament consists of books written by the people of the Old Covenant, under the inspiration of the Holy Spirit, to show God at work in nature and history.

Q. What is the New Testament?
A. The New Testament consists of books written by the people of the New Covenant, under the inspiration of the Holy Spirit, to set forth the life and teachings of Jesus and to proclaim the Good News of the Kingdom for all people.

Q. What is the Apocrypha?
A. The Apocrypha is a collection of additional books written by people of the Old Covenant, and used in the Christian Church.

Q. Why do we call the Holy Scriptures the Word of God?
A. We call them the Word of God because God inspired their human authors and because God still speaks to us through the Bible.

Q. How do we understand the meaning of the Bible?
A. We understand the meaning of the Bible by the help of the Holy Spirit, who guides the Church in the true interpretation of the Scriptures.

The Church

Q. What is the Church?
A. The Church is the community of the New Covenant.

Q. How is the Church described in the Bible?
A. The Church is described as the Body of which Jesus Christ is the Head and of which all baptized persons are members. It is called the People of God, the New Israel, a holy nation, a royal priesthood, and the pillar and ground of truth.

Q. How is the Church described in the creeds?
A. The Church is described as one, holy, catholic, and apostolic.

Q. Why is the Church described as one?
A. The Church is one, because it is one Body, under one Head, our Lord Jesus Christ.

Q. Why is the Church described as holy?
A. The Church is holy, because the Holy Spirit dwells in it, consecrates its members, and guides them to do God's work.

Q. Why is the Church described as catholic?
A. The Church is catholic, because it proclaims the whole Faith to all people, to the end of time.

Q. Why is the Church described as apostolic?
A. The Church is apostolic, because it continues in the teaching and fellowship of the apostles and is sent to carry out Christ's mission to all people.

Q. What is the mission of the Church?
A. The mission of the Church is to restore all people to unity with God and each other in Christ.

Q. How does the Church pursue its mission?
A. The Church pursues its mission as it prays and worships, proclaims the Gospel, and promotes justice, peace, and love.

Q. Through whom does the Church carry out its mission?
A. The church carries out its mission through the ministry of all its members.

The Ministry

Q. Who are the ministers of the Church?
A. The ministers of the Church are laypersons, bishops, priests, and deacons.

Q. What is the ministry of the laity?
A. The ministry of lay persons is the represent Christ and his Church; to bear witness to him wherever they may be; and, according to the gifts given them, to carry on Christ's work of reconciliation in the world; and to take their place in the life, worship, and governance of the Church.

Q. What is the ministry of a bishop?
A. The ministry of a bishop is to represent Christ and his Church, particularly as apostle, chief priest, and pastor of a diocese; to guard the faith, unity, and discipline of the whole Church; to proclaim the Word of God; to act in Christ's name for the reconciliation of the world and the building up of the Church; and to ordain others to continue Christ's ministry.

Q. What is the ministry of a priest or presbyter?
A. The ministry of a priest is to represent Christ and his Church, particularly as pastor to the people; to share with the bishop in the overseeing of the Church; to proclaim the Gospel; to administer the sacraments; and to bless and declare pardon in the name of God.

Q. What is the ministry of a deacon?
A. The ministry of a deacon is to represent Christ and his Church, particularly as a servant of those in need; and to assist bishops and priests in the proclamation of the Gospel and the administration of the sacraments.

Q. What is the duty of all Christians?
A. The duty of all Christians is to follow Christ; to come together week by week for corporate worship; and to work, pray, and give for the spread of the kingdom of God.

Prayer and Worship

Q. What is prayer?
A. Prayer is responding to God, by thought and by deeds, with or without words.

Q. What is Christian Prayer?
A. Christian prayer is response of God the Father, through Jesus Christ, in the power of the Holy Spirit.

Q. What prayer did Christ teach us?
A. Our Lord gave us the example of prayer knows as the Lord's Prayer.

The Lord's Prayer
Our Father, who art in heaven,
hallowed be thy Name,
thy kingdom come,
thy will be done,
on earth as it is in heaven.
Give us this day our daily bread.
And forgive us our trespasses,
as we forgive those
who trespass against us.
And lead us not into temptation,
but deliver us from evil.
For thine is the kingdom,
and the power, and the glory,
for ever and ever. Amen.

Q. What are the principle kinds of prayer?
A. The principle kinds of prayer are adoration, praise, thanksgiving, penitence, oblation, intercession, and petition.

Q. What is adoration?
A. Adoration is the lifting up of the heart and mind to God, asking nothing but to enjoy God's presence.

Q. Why do we praise God?
A. We praise God, not to obtain anything, but because God's Being draws praise from us.

Q. For what do we offer thanksgiving?
A. Thanksgiving is offered to God for all the blessings of this life, for our redemption, and for whatever draws us closer to God.

Q. What is penitence?
A. In penitence, we confess our sins and make restitution where possible, with the intention to amend our lives.

Q. What is prayer of oblation?
A. Oblation is an offering of ourselves, our lives and labors, in union with Christ, for the purposes of God.

Q. What are intercession and petition?
A. Intercession brings before God the needs of others; in petition, we present our own needs, that God's will may be done.

Q. What is corporate worship?
A. In corporate worship, we unite ourselves with others to acknowledge the holiness of God, to hear God's Word, to offer prayer, and to celebrate the sacraments.

The Sacraments

Q. What are the sacraments?
A. The sacraments are outward and visible signs of inward and spiritual grace, given by Christ as sure and certain means by which we receive that grace.

Q. What is grace?
A. Grace is God's favor toward us, unearned and undeserved; by grace God forgives our sins, enlightens our minds, stirs our hearts, and strengthens our wills.

Q. What are the two great sacraments of the Gospel?
A. The two great sacraments given by Christ to his Church are Holy Baptism and the Holy Eucharist.

Holy Baptism

Q. What is Holy Baptism?
A. Holy Baptism is the sacrament by which God adopts us as his children and makes us members of Christ's Body, the Church, and inheritors of the kingdom of God.

Q. What is the outward and visible sign in Baptism?
A. The outward and visible sign in Baptism is water, in which the person is baptized in the Name of the Father, and of the Son, and of the Holy Spirit.

Q. What is the inward and spiritual grace in Baptism?
A. The inward and spiritual grace in Baptism is union with Christ in his death and resurrection, birth into God's family the Church, forgiveness of sins, and new life in the Holy Spirit.

Q. What is required of us at Baptism?
A. It is required that we renounce Satan, repent of our sins, and accept Jesus as our Lord and Savior.

Q. Why then are infants baptized?
A. Infants are baptized so that they can share citizenship in the Covenant, membership in Christ, and redemption by God.

Q. How are the promises for infants made and carried out?
A. Promises are made for them by their parents and sponsors, who guarantee that the infants will be brought up within the Church, to know Christ and be able to follow him.

The Holy Eucharist

Q. What is the Holy Eucharist?
A. The Holy Eucharist is the sacrament commanded by Christ for the continual remembrance of his life, death, and resurrection, until his coming again.

Q. Why is the Eucharist called a sacrifice?
A. Because the Eucharist, the Church's sacrifice of praise and thanksgiving, is the way by which the sacrifice of Christ is made present, and in which he unites us to his one offering of himself.``

Q. By what other names is this service known?
A. The Holy Eucharist is called the Lord's Supper, and Holy Communion; it is also known as the Divine Liturgy, the Mass, and the Great Offering.

Q. What is the outward and visible sign in the Eucharist?
A. The outward and visible sign in the Eucharist is bread and wine, give and received according to Christ's command.

Q. What is the inward and spiritual grace given in the Eucharist?
A. The inward and spiritual grace in the Holy Communion is the Body and Blood of Christ give to his people, and received by faith.

Q. What are the benefits which we receive in the Lord's Supper?
A. The benefits we receive are the forgiveness of our sins, the strengthening of our union with Christ and one another, and the foretaste of the heavenly banquet which is our nourishment in eternal life.

Q. What is required of us when we come to the Eucharist?
A. It is required that we should examine our lives, repent of our sins, and be in love and charity with all people.

Other Sacramental Rites

Q. What other sacramental rites evolved in the Church under the guidance of the Holy Spirit?
A. Other sacramental rites which evolved in the Church include confirmation, ordination, holy matrimony, reconciliation of a penitent, and unction.

Q. How do they differ from the two sacraments of the Gospel?
A. Although they are means of grace, they are not necessary for all persons in the same way that Baptism and the Eucharist are.

Q. What is Confirmation?
A. Confirmation is the rite in which we express a mature commitment to Christ, and receive strength from the Holy Spirit through prayer and the laying on of hands by a bishop.

Q. What is required of those to be confirmed?
A. It is required of those to be confirmed that they have been baptized, are sufficiently instructed in the Christian Faith, are penitent for their sins, and are ready to affirm their confession of Jesus Christ as Savior and Lord.

Q. What is Ordination?
A. Ordination is the rite in which God gives authority and the grace of the Holy Spirit to those being made bishops, priests, and deacons, through prayer and the laying on of hands by bishops.

Q. What is Holy Matrimony?
A. Holy Matrimony is Christian marriage, in which the woman and man enter into a life-long union, make their vows before God and the Church, and receive the grace and blessing of God to help them fulfill their vows.

Q. What is Reconciliation of a Penitent?
A. Reconciliation of a Penitent, or Penance, is the rite in which those who repent of their sins may confess them to God in the presence of a priest, and receive the assurance of pardon and the grace of absolution.

Q. What is Unction of the Sick?
A. Unction is the rite of anointing the sick with oil, or the laying on of hands, by which God's grace is given for the healing of spirit, mind, and body.

Q. Is God's activity limited to these rites?
A. God does not limit himself to these rites; they are patterns of countless ways by which God uses material things to reach out to us.

Q. How are the sacraments related to our Christian hope?
A. Sacraments sustain our present hope and anticipate its future fulfillment.

The Christian Hope

Q. What is the Christian hope?
A. The Christian hope is to live with confidence in newness and fullness of life, and to await the coming of Christ in glory, and the completion of God's purpose for the world.

Q. What do we mean by the coming of Christ in glory?
A. By the coming of Christ in glory, we mean that Christ will come, not in weakness but in power, and will make all things new.

Q. What do we mean by heaven and hell?
A. By heaven, we mean eternal life in our enjoyment of God; by hell, we mean eternal death in our rejection of God.

Q. Why do we pray for the dead?
A. We pray for them, because we still hold them in our love, and because we trust that in God's presence those who have chosen to serve him will grow in his love, until they see him as he is.

Q. What do we mean by the last judgment?
A. We believe that Christ will come in glory and judge the living and the dead.

Q. What do we mean by the resurrection of the body?
A. We mean that God will raise us from death in the fullness of our being, that we may live with Christ in the communion of the saints.

Q. What is the communion of saints?
A. The communion of saints is the whole family of God, the living and the dead, those whom we love and those whom we hurt, bound together in Christ by sacrament, prayer, and praise.

Q. What do we mean by everlasting life?
A. By everlasting life, we mean a new existence, in which we are united with all the people of God, in the joy of fully knowing and loving God and each other.

Q. What, then, is our assurance as Christians?
A. Our assurance as Christians is that nothing, not even death, shall separate us from the love of God which is in Christ Jesus our Lord. Amen.

The Creeds

The Apostles' Creed
I believe in God, the Father almighty,
   creator of heaven and earth;
I believe in Jesus Christ, his only Son, our Lord.
   He was conceived by the power of the Holy Spirit
      and born of the Virgin Mary.
   He suffered under Pontius Pilate,
      was crucified, died, and was buried.
   He descended to the dead.
   On the third day he rose again.
   He ascended into heaven,
      and is seated at the right hand of the Father.
   He will come again to judge the living and the dead.
I believe in the Holy Spirit,
   the holy catholic Church,
   the communion of saints,
   the forgiveness of sins
   the resurrection of the body,
   and the life everlasting. Amen.

The Nicene Creed
We believe in one God,
   the Father, the Almighty,
   maker of heaven and earth,
   of all that is, seen and unseen.
We believe in one Lord, Jesus Christ,
   the only Son of God,
   eternally begotten of the Father,
   God from God, Light from Light,
   true God from true God,
   begotten, not made,
   of one Being with the Father.
   Through him all things were made.
   For us and for our salvation
      by the power of the Holy Spirit

> he became incarnate from the Virgin Mary,
> and was made man.
> For our sake he was crucified under Pontius Pilate;
> he suffered death and was buried.
> On the third day he rose again
> in accordance with the Scriptures;
> he ascended into heaven
> and is seated at the right hand of the Father.
> He will come again in glory to judge the living and the dead,
> and his kingdom will have no end.
> We believe in the Holy Spirit, the Lord, the giver of life,
> who proceeds from the Father.
> With the Father and the Son he is worshiped and glorified.
> He has spoken through the Prophets.
> We believe in one holy catholic and apostolic Church.
> We acknowledge one baptism for the forgiveness of sins.
> We look for the resurrection of the dead,
> and the life of the world to come. Amen.

The Creed of Saint Athanasius

Whosoever will be saved, before all things it is necessary that he hold the Catholic Faith.

Which Faith except everyone do keep whole and undefiled, without doubt he shall perish everlastingly.

And the Catholic Faith is this: That we worship one God in Trinity, and Trinity in Unity, neither confounding the Persons, nor dividing the Substance.

For there is one Person of the Father, another of the Son, and another of the Holy Ghost.

But the Godhead of the Father, of the Son, and of the Holy Ghost, is all one, the Glory equal, the Majesty co-eternal.

Such as the Father is, such is the Son, and such is the Holy Ghost.

The Father uncreate, the Son uncreate, and the Holy Ghost uncreate.

The Father incomprehensible, the Son incomprehensible, and the Holy Ghost incomprehensible.

The Father eternal, the Son eternal, and the Holy Ghost eternal.

And yet they are not three eternals, but one eternal.

As also there are not three incomprehensibles, nor three uncreated, but

one uncreated, and one incomprehensible.
So likewise the Father is Almighty, the Son Almighty, and the Holy Ghost Almighty.
And yet they are not three Almighties, but one Almighty.
So the Father is God, the Son is God, and the Holy Ghost is God.
And yet they are not three Gods, but one God.
So likewise the Father is Lord, the Son Lord, and the Holy Ghost Lord.
And yet not three Lords, but one Lord.
For like as we are compelled by the Christian verity to acknowledge every Person by himself to be both God and Lord,
So are we forbidden by the Catholic Religion, to say, There be three Gods, or three Lords.
The Father is made of none, neither created, nor begotten.
The Son is of the Father alone, not made, nor created, but begotten.
The Holy Ghost is of the Father and of the Son, neither made, nor created, nor begotten, but proceeding.
So there is one Father, not three Fathers; one Son, not three Sons; one Holy Ghost, not three Holy Ghosts.
And in this Trinity none is afore, or after other; none is greater, or less than another;
But the whole three Persons are co-eternal together and co-equal.
So that in all things, as is aforesaid, the Unity in Trinity and the Trinity in Unity is to be worshipped.
He therefore that will be saved is must think thus of the Trinity.

Furthermore, it is necessary to everlasting salvation that he also believe rightly the Incarnation of our Lord Jesus Christ.
For the right Faith is, that we believe and confess, that our Lord Jesus Christ, the Son of God, is God and Man;
God, of the substance of the Father, begotten before the worlds; and Man of the substance of his Mother, born in the world;
Perfect God and perfect Man, of a reasonable soul and human flesh subsisting.
Equal to the Father, as touching his Godhead; and inferior to the Father, as touching his manhood;
Who, although he be God and Man, yet he is not two, but one Christ;
One, not by conversion of the Godhead into flesh but by taking of the Manhood into God;

One altogether; not by confusion of Substance, but by unity of Person. For as the reasonable soul and flesh is one man, so God and Man is one Christ;

Who suffered for our salvation, descended into hell, rose again the third day from the dead.

He ascended into heaven, he sitteth at the right hand of the Father, God Almighty, from whence he will come to judge the quick and the dead. At whose coming all men will rise again with their bodies and shall give account for their own works.

And they that have done good shall go into life everlasting; and they that have done evil into everlasting fire.

This is the Catholic Faith, which except a man believe faithfully, he cannot be saved.

THE DIDACHE
*Translated from the Greek text published
by Roswell D. Hitchcock in 1884.*

TEACHING OF THE LORD TO THE NATIONS THROUGH THE TWELVE APOSTLES

ONE

Two ways there are, one of life and one of death, but there is a great difference between the two ways.
The way of life is indeed this: First, you will love the God who made you; secondly, "you will love your neighbor as yourself." Now all the things that you do not want to have happen to you, you too do not do *these* to one another.

Now the teaching of these sayings is this: "Praise those who curse you", and pray for your enemies; now fast for those who are persecuting you. For what favor is it if you love those who love you? Don't the gentiles do the same? But you love those who hate you, and you will have no enemies.

"Hold yourself away from the fleshly" and kosmic "strong desires." "If someone should give you a blow to your right cheek, turn to him also the left one," and you will be complete. "If anyone should force you to go one mile, go with him two." "If anyone takes your cloak, give him your tunic also." If anyone takes what is yours away from you, do not ask for it back. For neither are you able. "Give to everyone who asks from you," and do not ask for it back. For the Father wants to give of his own free gifts to everyone.

Blessed is the one who gives according to the precept, for he is guiltless. Woe to the one who takes. For if indeed someone takes who has a need, he will be guiltless. But the one who has no need will give a judgment as to why he took, and for what *reason*, and he will come under arrest and will be examined about what he did. And "he will not go out from there until he pays the last quadrans." But it has also been said about this: "Let your charitable gifts sweat in your hands, until indeed you know who to give to."

Now the second precept of the teaching is: "You will not murder. You will not commit adultery." You will not sodomize young boys. You will not have unlawful sex. "You will not steal." Do not practice magic. Do not practice sorcery. Neither murder a child by abortion, nor will you destroy what is born. You will not strongly desire your neighbor's things. You will not make oaths. " You will not bear false testimony." You will not say bad things. You will not remember bad things. You will not be double-minded or double-tongued, for the double-tongue is a snare of death. Your message is not to be false or empty, but being filled with practice. You should be neither greedy nor a swindler, nor hypocrite, nor malicious, nor high-minded. You will not take evil counsel against your neighbor. You will not hate any people, but you will reprove some, and you will pray for some, and some you will love more than your life.

    My child, flee from every evil thing, and from everything like it. Do not become angry, for anger is the way to murder. Neither should you be jealous, nor *one who creates* strife, nor emotional. For murders are born out of all of these.

    My child, do not become strongly desirous, for strong desire is the way to sexual sin. Neither should you be a speaker of filth, nor high-eyed. For adulteries are born out of all of these.

    My child, do not become someone who looks for omens, since it is the way to idolatry. Neither should you be an enchanter, nor an astrologer, nor a cleanser. Nor should you want to look at these things, for idolatry is born out of all of these things.

    My child, do not become a liar, since lying is the way to theft. Neither should you be greedy, nor a lover of money, nor worthlessly conceited. For thefts are born out of all of these things. My child, do not become a grumbler, since it leads to evil speaking. Neither should you be assumers, nor evil-minded. For evil-speakings are born out of all of these.

    But be meek, since "the meek will inherit the land." Become longsuffering, and merciful, and guiltless, and quiet, and good, and throughout everything tremble at the sayings that you have heard. You will not exalt yourself, nor will you give *over-boldness* to your soul. Your soul will not cling with the high people, but you will conduct yourself with the just and lowly ones. Accept the things that transpire to you as good workings, knowing that nothing happens without God.

    My child, remember night and day the one who is speaking God's message to you. Now you will honor him as *you would honor* the Lord. For where the lordship may be spoken, there is the Lord. Now daily you will seek out the faces of the holy ones, so that you would be refreshed by their words. You will not want division, but you will make peace with those who are fighting. You will judge justly. In giving a reproof of a wandering, you will not respect *anyone's* presence. You will not be two souled regarding whether or not it should be. Do not become *like* one who stretches out his hands for taking but who draws them in for giving. If you have, you will give by your hands a ransom for your sins. You will not hesitate to give, nor will you grumble while giving. For you will know who it is that is the nice payer of the reward. You will not turn away the one who is needy, but you will share all things together with your brother, and you will not claim them to be your own things. For if you are partners in what is immortal, how much more *are you partners* in what is mortal?

You will not take your hand away from your son or your daughter, but from youth you will teach the fear of God. You will not give directives in your bitterness to your slave or handmaid, these who are hoping in the same God. Otherwise they may not fear the God who is *over* both of you. For he is not coming to call *people* according to *appearance*, but upon those whom the spirit has made ready. Now you who are slaves should be submissive to your lords in sobriety and fear, as to a type of God.

You will hate every hypocrisy and all of what is not pleasing to the Lord. You will by no means forsake the Lord's precepts, but you will guard what you have received--neither adding to them nor removing from *them*. You will acknowledge your wanderings in an assembly, and you will not come forward to your prayer with an evil consciousness. This is the way of life.

TWO

Now the way of death is this: First of all, it is evil and full of curses: murders, adulteries, strong desires, unlawful sex acts, thefts, idolatries, magic acts, sorceries, robberies, false testimonies, hypocrisies, two-heartedness, deceit, arrogance, badness, assumptions, greed, shameful speech, jealousy, an overbearing nature, loftiness, pride; persecutors of good; hating truth, loving falsehood; not knowing the reward of what is right, not clinging to good, nor to just judgment, watching not for good but for evil. Far from these *people* are meekness and endurance. *They* love worthless things, persuing revenge, not showing mercy to a poor person, not laboring for those who are weary, not knowing the one who made them, murderers of children, corrupters of molded image of God, turning away those who are in need, oppressing the afflicted; comforters of the wealthy, lawless judges of the poor; universal sinners. Children, may you be rescued from all of these.

See to it that no one lead you astray from this way of the teaching, since it does not teach you without God. For if indeed you are able to bear the whole of the Lord's yoke, you will be complete. But if you are not able, do what you are able.

THREE

Now about food: bear what you are able to bear. But watch out for the idol-sacrifices, for this is a religious service of dead gods.

Now about baptism, baptize this way: after first uttering all of these things, baptize "into the name of the Father and of the son and of the holy Spirit" in running water. But if you do not have running water, baptize in other water. Now if you are not able to *do so* in cold *water, do it* in warm water. Now if you don't have either, pour water three times on the head, "into the name of the Father, and of the son, and of the holy Spirit." Now before the ritual cleansing, the baptizer and the one being baptized should fast, and any others who are able. Now you will give word for the one who is being baptized to fast for one or two *days* beforehand.

But do not let your fasts be with the hypocrites. For they fast on the second day of the week and on the fifth. But you fast on the fourth day and the day of preparation. Neither should you pray like the hypocrites, but as the Lord gave word in his good message, pray like this: "Our Father, the one who is in Heaven, your name has been made holy. Let your kingdom come. Let what you want also be done on earth, as in Heaven. Give us the bread we need today and forgive us our debts as we also forgive our debtors. And don't carry us into trial, but rescue us from the evil one. For yours is the power and the glory for the age." Pray this way three times daily.

Now about the thanksgiving, give thanks this way:

First, about the cup: "We thank you, our Father, for the holy vine of your boy David which you made known to us through your boy Jesus. Glory be to you for the age.
Now about the broken *loaf*: "We thank you, our Father, for the life and the knowledge that you made known to us through your boy Jesus. Glory be to you for the age. Just as this broken *loaf* was scattered on top of the hills and as it was gathered together and became one, in the same way let your assembly be gathered together from the remotest parts of the land into your kingdom. "For yours is the glory and the power through Anointed Jesus for the age." Now no one should either eat or drink from your thanksgiving meal, but those who have been baptized into the Lord's name. For about this also the Lord said, "Do not give what is holy to the dogs."
Now after you have been filled, give thanks this way: "We thank you, holy Father, for your holy name, which you made to live in our hearts, and for the knowledge and trust and immortality which you made known to us through Jesus your boy. Glory be to you for the age. "Almighty master, it was you who created all for the sake of your name. You gave both food and drink to people for enjoyment, so that they might give thanks to you. But to us you have freely given spiritual food and drink and eternal life through your boy. Before all things, we are thankful to you that you are powerful. Glory be to you for the age.

"O Lord, remember your assembly, *remember* to rescue it from every evil and to make it complete in your love, and to gather it from the four winds into your kingdom which you prepared for it--*it*, which has been made holy. For yours is the power and the glory for the age.

"Let generosity come, and let this universe pass away. Hosanna to David's son! If someone is holy, let him come. If someone is not, he should change his mind. Marana-tha. A-mein." Now permit the prophets to give thanks as much as they want.

FOUR

Therefore, the one who comes and teaches you all of these things which have been previously spoken, accept him. But if he, the teacher, should turn to teach another teaching, so as to release *this* one, do not listen to him. But if *he teaches* to promote what is right and knowledge of the Lord, accept him as *you would* the Lord.

Now about the envoys and prophets, do just as according to the tenet of the good message. Now each envoy who comes to you, accept as *you would* the Lord. But he will not remain for one day. Now if there is need, also the next *day*. But if he remains for three, he is a false prophet.

Now when the envoy departs, he should take nothing except bread until he lodges. But if he should ask for money, he is a false prophet.

And every prophet who speaks with the spirit, you will not test or judge, for every sin will be forgiven. But not everyone who speaks with the spirit is a prophet: but if he has the conduct of the Lord. Therefore, from *their* conduct, the false prophet and the prophet will be made known. And no prophet with the spirit who orders a meal eats from it, unless indeed he is a false prophet. Now every prophet who teaches the truth, if he does not do as he teaches, is a false prophet. But every prophet who has been proved, who is true, who does things for the kosmic secrets of the assembly but who does not teach to do as he does, will not be judged among you. For the ancient prophets did it this way also. But whoever says with the spirit, "Give me money (or something else)," you will not listen to him. But if he says to give on behalf of others who are in need, no one should judge him.

Now everyone who comes in the Lord's name should be accepted. But afterward, you will examine him to know him. For you will have understanding, right and left. If the one who comes is a traveller, help him as much as you are able. But he will not remain with you except for two or three days, if there is a necessity. But if he wants to dwell with you, since he is a craftsman, he should work to eat. But if he has no craft, provide according to your understanding, so that no lazy person would be lifing among you *as* an "Anointed". But if he does not want to do this, he is one who profits financially from the Anointed One. Be careful about such people.

Now every true prophet who wants to settle near you is worthy of his wage. In the same way, a true teacher is also worthy, just as the workman, of his wage. Therefore, every foremost part of the products of the press and threshing floor, both of oxen and of sheep, you will take and give to the prophets. For they are your high priests.

But if you do not have a prophet, give *these* to the poor. If you make baked bread, take the foremost part and give according to the precept. In the same way, when you open a jar of wine or of oil, take the foremost part and give to the prophets. Now of money and clothing and every possession, take the foremost part as you think it right and give according to the precept.

FIVE

Now according to the Lord's *day*, gather together and break bread and give thanks, after acknowledging your wanderings to *one another*, so your sacrifice would be a clean one. But each one who has something against his friend, do not let him come together with you until they are reconciled, so that your sacrifice would not be made common. For this is what was declared by the Lord: "In every place and time, carry to me a clean sacrifice. Because I am a great king," says Yahweh, "and my name is a wondrous thing among the nations."

SIX

Now hand pick for yourselves overseers and servants worthy of the Lord: men who are meek, not lovers of money, true and proved. For they are giving religious service to you also, as the prophets and teachers are giving religious service.

SEVEN

Now reprove one another, not in anger but in peace, as you have it in the good message. And no one should speak to each one who misses the mark against another one, nor should he hear from you, until he changes his mind. But your vows and your charitable works and all your practices, do these, as you have it in the good message of our Lord.

Be vigilant on behalf of your life. Do not let your lamps be extinguished, and do not relax your loins. But become prepared. For you do not know the hour in which our Lord is coming. Now you will gather together often, seeking the things that are appropriate for your souls. For all the time of your trust will not profit you, if you do not become complete in the last season.

For in the last days, the false prophets and the corruptors will be multiplied, and the sheep will be turned into wolves, and love will be turned into hate. For when the lawlessness increases, they will hate one another, and they will persecute and deliver up, and then the deceiver of creation will appear as God's son, and he will do signs and wonders. And the land will be given up into his hands. And he will do lawless things which have never been done from the age.

Then human creation will come into the fire of examination, and many will stumble and be destroyed. But those who endure in their trust will be saved from this accursed thing. And then the signs of truth will appear. First, the sign of an opening in Heaven, then the sign of a trumpet's sound, and thirdly, a resurrection of dead people. But not of all people; on the contrary, as it was declared, "The Lord will come, and all the holy ones with him." Then creation will see the Lord "coming on the clouds of the sky."

Fourteen Theses of the Old Catholic Church

1. We agree that the apocryphal or deutero-canonical books of the Old Testament are not of the same canonicity as the books contained in the Hebrew Canon.
2. We agree that no translation of Holy Scripture can claim an authority superior to that of the original text.
3. We agree that the reading of Holy Scripture in the vulgar tongue cannot be lawfully forbidden.
4. We agree that, in general, it is more fitting, and in accordance with the spirit of the Church, that the Liturgy should be in the tongue understood by the people.
5. We agree that Faith working by Love, not Faith without Love, is the means and condition of Man's justification before God.
6. Salvation cannot be merited by "merit of condignity," because there is no proportion between the infinite worth of salvation promised by God and the finite worth of man's works.
7. We agree that the doctrine of "opera supererogationis" and of a "thesaurus meritorium sanctorum," i.e., that the overflowing merits of the Saints can be transferred to others, either by the rulers of the Church, or by the authors of the good works themselves, is untenable.
8. We acknowledge that the number of sacraments was fixed at seven, first in the twelfth century, and then was received into the general teaching of the Church, not as a tradition coming down from the Apostles or from the earliest of times, but as the result of theological speculation. 2. Catholic theologians acknowledge, and we acknowledge with them, that Baptism and the Eucharist are "principalia, praecipus, eximia salutis nostrae sacramenta."
9. The Holy Scriptures being recognized as the primary rule of Faith, we agree that the genuine tradition, i.e. the unbroken transmission partly oral, partly in writing of the doctrine delivered by Christ and the Apostles is an authoritative source of teaching for all successive generations of Christians. This tradition is partly to be found in the consensus of the great ecclesiastical bodies standing in historical continuity with the primitive Church, partly to be gathered by scientific method from the written documents of all centuries. 2. We acknowledge that the Church of England; and the Churches

derived through her, have maintained unbroken the Episcopal succession.
10. We reject the new Roman doctrine of the Immaculate Conception of the Blessed Virgin Mary, as being contrary to the tradition of the first thirteen centuries, according to which Christ alone is conceived without sin.
11. We agree that the practice of confession of sins before the congregation or a Priest, together with the exercise of the power of the keys, has come down to us from the primitive Church, and that, purged from abuses and free from constraint, it should be preserved in the Church.
12. We agree that "indulgences" can only refer to penalties actually imposed by the Church herself.
13. We acknowledge that the practice of the commemoration of the faithful departed, i.e. the calling down of a richer outpouring of Christ's grace upon them, has come down to us from the primitive Church, and is to be preserved in the Church.
14. The Eucharistic celebration in the Church is not a continuous repetition or renewal of the propitiatory sacrifice offered once forever by Christ upon the cross; but its sacrificial character consists in this, that it is the permanent memorial of it, and a representation and presentation on earth of that one oblation of Christ for the salvation of redeemed mankind, which according to the Epistle to the Hebrews (9:11,12), is continuously presented in heaven by Christ, who now appears in the presence of God for us (9:24). 2. While this is the character of the Eucharist in reference to the sacrifice of Christ, it is also a sacred feast, wherein the faithful, receiving the Body and Blood of our Lord, have communion one with another (I Cor. 10:17).

Declaration of Utrecht

We adhere faithfully to the Rule of Faith laid down by St. Vincent of Lerins in these terms: "Id teneamus, quod ubique, quod semper, quod ab omnibus creditum est; hoc est etenim vere proprieque catholicum." For this reason we preserve in professing the faith of the primitive Church, as formulated in the oecumenical symbols and specified precisely by the unanimously accepted decisions of the Oecumenical Councils held in the undivided Church of the first thousand years.
We therefore reject the decrees of the so-called Council of the Vatican, which were promulgated July 18th, 1870, concerning the infallibility and the universal Episcopate of the Bishop of Rome, decrees which are in contradiction with the faith of the ancient Church, and which destroy its ancient canonical constitution by attributing to the Pope the plentitude of ecclesiastical powers over all Dioceses and over all the faithful. By denial of this primatial jurisdiction we do not wish to deny the historical primacy which several Oecumenical Councils and Fathers of the ancient Church have attributed to the Bishop of Rome by recognizing him as the Primus inter pares. We also reject the dogma of the Immaculate Conception promulgated by Pius IX in 1854 in defiance of the Holy Scriptures and in contradiction to the tradition of the centuries.
As for other Encyclicals published by the Bishops of Rome in recent times for example, the Bulls Unigenitus and Auctorem fidei , and the Syllabus of 1864, we reject them on all such points as are in contradiction with the doctrine of the primitive Church, and we do not recognize them as binding on the consciences of the faithful. We also renew the ancient protests of the Catholic Church of Holland against the errors of the Roman Curia, and against its attacks upon the rights of national Churches.
We refuse to accept the decrees of the Council of Trent in matters of discipline, and as for the dogmatic decisions of that Council we accept them only so far as they are in harmony with the teaching of the primitive Church.
Considering that the Holy Eucharist has always been the true central point of Catholic worship, we consider it our right to declare that we maintain with perfect fidelity the ancient Catholic doctrine concerning the Sacrament of the Altar, by believing that we receive the Body and

Blood of our Saviour Jesus Christ under the species of bread and wine. The Eucharistic celebration in the Church is neither a continual repetition nor a renewal of the expiatory sacrifice which Jesus offered once for all upon the Cross: but it is a sacrifice because it is the perpetual commemoration of the sacrifice offered upon the Cross, and it is the act by which we represent upon earth and appropriate to ourselves the one offering which Jesus Christ makes in Heaven, according to the Epistle to the Hebrews 9:11-12, for the salvation of redeemed humanity, by appearing for us in the presence of God (Heb. 9:24). The character of the Holy Eucharist being thus understood, it is, at the same time, a sacrificial feast, by means of which the faithful in receiving the Body and Blood of our Saviour, enter into communion with one another (I Cor. 10:17).

We hope that Catholic theologians, in maintaining the faith of the undivided Church, will succeed in establishing an agreement upon questions which have been controverted ever since the divisions which arose between the Churches. We exhort the priests under our jurisdiction to teach, both by preaching and by the instruction of the young, especially the essential Christian truths professed by all the Christian confessions, to avoid, in discussing controverted doctrines, any violation of truth or charity, and in word and deed to set an example to the members.

By maintaining and professing faithfully the doctrine of Jesus Christ, by refusing to admit those errors which by the fault of men have crept into the Catholic Church, by laying aside the abuses in ecclesiastical matters, together with the worldly tendencies of the hierarchy, we believe that we shall be able to combat efficaciously the great evils of our day, which are unbelief and indifference in matters of religion.

Utrecht, 24th September 1889 - +Heykamp- +Rinkel - +Diependaal - +Reinkens -+Herzog

A Historic Overview of the Old Catholic Churches
by The Most Rev. Francis P. Facione

It seems appropriate to begin this discussion with a statement of what the Old Catholic Church is not. It is not a sect or a schism as some of its self-appointed critics may claim. The Old Catholic Church is a body of Christians committed to the Person of Jesus Christ and His teaching and, as shall become evident in this article, forms an historic part of the One, Holy, Catholic and Apostolic Church.

The Old Catholic Church affirms its historic continuity with the Apostolic Church of the first century through the ancient See of Utrecht in Holland. St. Willibrord, the Apostle of the Netherlands was consecrated to the Episcopacy by Pope Sergius I in 696 A.D. at Rome. Upon his return to the Netherlands, he established his See at Utrecht. In addition, he established the dioceses at Deventer and Haarlem. One of his successors was St. Boniface, the Apostle of Germany. The Church of Utrecht also provided a worthy occupant for the Papal See in 1552 in the person of Pope Hadrian VI, while two of the most able exponents of the spiritual life, Geert Groote, who founded the Brothers of the Common Life, and Thomas a Kempis, who is credited with writing the Imitation of Christ, were both from the Dutch Church.

Assenting to a petition made by the Holy Roman Emperor, Conrad II and Bishop Heribert of Utrecht, Blessed Pope Eugene III, in the year 1145 A.D., granted the Cathedral Chapter of Utrecht the right to elect successors to the See in times of vacancy. This privilege was affirmed by the Fourth Council of the Lateran in 1215. The autonomous character of the Ancient Catholic Church in the Netherlands was further demonstrated when a second papal grant by Pope Leo X, Debitum Pastoralis, conceded to Philip of Burgundy, the 57th Bishop of Utrecht, that neither he nor any of his successors, nor any of their clergy or laity, should ever, in the first instance, have his cause evoked to an external tribunal, not even under pretense of any apostolic letters whatever; and all such proceedings should be, ipso facto, null and void. This papal concession, in 1520, was of the greatest importance in the defense of the rights of the Church of Utrecht.

Armed with the protection of the papal concessions, the Church in the netherlands continued to minister even through the turbulence of the Reformation. During this period of strife, the Church in the Netherlands, as in many other countries, was forced to "go underground" in order to survive and remain intact, it did. Eventually, the Archbishop of Utrecht and other church leaders reached informal agreement with the civil government whereby it could again function openly without interference from the Reformers.

While peace and toleration was achieved with the civil government, a new, growing tension was developing for the Church in Utrecht. The cause of this uneasiness was the motivation of the Counter-Reformers, most notably the Jesuits, to "re- missionize" the Dutch Church. In 1592, the Jesuits, for reasons largely political, began to invade the jurisdiction of the Archbishop of Utrecht, and although more than once rebuked by the Pope and ordered to submit themselves to the authority of the Archbishop, their machinations continued unabated. This intrusion of the Counter-Reformers was strongly resisted by the clergy and bishops of the Netherlands as well as frowned upon by the Dutch government. Nevertheless, in 1691, the Jesuits took the step of falsely accusing the Archbishop, Petter Codde, of favoring the so-called Jansenist heresy. The Holy Father, Pope Innocent XII appointed a Commission of Cardinals to investigate the accusations against Archbishop Codde. The result of this inquiry was a complete and unconditional exoneration of the Archbishop.

Undaunted by the decision of the Commission appointed by Pope Innocent XII, the Counter-Reformers prevailed upon the new Pope, Clement XI, to summon Archbishop Codde to Rome in 1700 under the pretext of participating in the Jubilee Year whereupon a second Commission was appointed to try the Archbishop. The result of this second proceeding was again a complete and unconditional acquittal. While this should have ended the matter, it didn't. Pope Clement was prevailed upon to issue an order which suspended the Archbishop in 1701 and appointed a successor to the See of Utrecht.

When news of these events was made public, the indignation, even on the part of those most favorable to the Counter-Reformers' position was unbound. Believing the suspension of their Archbishop to be an unprecedented injustice, those left in charge refused to acquiesce in it, and maintained not only the wrongfulness of the action, but also their unassailable right to choose a successor to Codde, and refused to recognize the person whom Pope Clement wished to thrust upon them. In this stance, they were joined by many theologians and canon lawyers as well as bishops and civil officials including the Dutch Government which not only refused to allow Archbishop Codde's "successor" to function in Holland, but also demanded that Codde be allowed to return to Utrecht.

Upon his return to Utrecht in June of 1703, Archbishop Codde found everything in the wildest confusion. Continued conflict seemed inevitable as attempts to resolve the matter were useless. Finally, in a Pastoral Letter of 19 March 1704, Codde announced his decision to retire from the actual exercise of his office, under protest against the injustice of his suspension. He retired to his country house near Utrecht where he died on December 18, 1710.

With Archbishop Codde's decision to retire, the administration of the diocese reverted, according to all principles of canon law, to the Cathedral Chapter which ably discharged its duties. During this period, the chapter arranged to have an Irish bishop, Luke Fagan, Bishop of Meath and later Archbishop of Dublin, ordain priests for the Church of Utrecht. Following Luke Fagan's lead, three French bishops also signified their willingness to ordain clergy for the Dutch church.

Meanwhile, the oppressed Church continued its efforts to obtain a hearing for resolution of its grievances. Its case was presented to the University of Louvain in May of 1717. In the course of that year and the next, the entire body of theologians and canonists of the University agreed that the rights of the Chapter of Utrecht had been violated and the actions against it were not only contrary to church law but null and void. Its appeal to a future General Council of the Church was ignored. As a result, the Church of Holland which had been, de jure, autonomous, became, de facto, an independent Catholic church.

Thus was the situation to remain until 1723 when on April 27th, the Cathedral Chapter proceeded to the election of the Seventh Archbishop of Utrecht, Dr. Cornelius Steenoven, who had been the companion of Archbishop Codde during his sojourn at Rome. Steenoven was consecrated to the episcopacy on October 15, 1724 by Monsignor Dominique Varlet, Bishop of Ascalon, then resident in Amsterdam because of his own difficulties with Counter-Reformers and others intriguing against him. Bishop Varlet was to be called upon to consecrate three other archbishops for Utrecht between 1724 and 1739. He died at the Hague on May 14, 1742.

The Tenth Archbishop, Peter John Meindaerts, consecrated by Varlet on St. Luke's Day, 1739, proceeded to the consecration of Jerome de Bock for the diocese of Haarlem thus assuring the episcopacy for the Church of Holland following Varlet's death.

The question of a third bishop had long occupied the attention of Archbishop Meindaerts. After much discussion and considerable delays, the Archbishop and Canons assembled in September, 1757 and elected Bartholomew John Byevelt, one of the Canons, Bishop of Deventer. He was consecrated bishop on the Conversion of St. Paul, January 25, 1758.

In 1763, at the call of Archbishop Meindaerts, a synod of the bishops and clergy was held, and the acts of this synod are a remarkable testimony to its firm hold of the Faith, and its intention that the church of Holland should remain steadfast in it. With the publication of these acts in other countries, there was considerable hope that a medium had been found to heal the breach between Rome and the church of Holland. Unfortunately, these hopes were destined to remain unfulfilled and the church of Holland continued in its forced state of isolation.

In 1853, Pope Pius IX established a rival hierarchy to that of the church of Holland, and so now there were two churches of Holland, both catholic, rivals, though not actually enemies. It was this "restoration" of the hierarchy which gave rise to the name "Old Roman Catholic" which began to be applied to the original Church to distinguish it from the new establishment of Pius IX.

In 1870, Pope Pius IX convened Vatican Council I, enriching the hope of the church of Holland that it would receive a hearing on its grievances. Alas this was not to be as its bishops were refused seating in the deliberations of that synod. In fact, at the instigation of those unfavorable to the cause of the church of Holland, the Vatican Council abolished the principle of appeal to a general council of the Church.

Following the Vatican Council I, a considerable dissent among Catholics in parts of Germany, Austria and Switzerland arose over the issue of the definition of papal infallibility as a dogma of the Church. The dissenters, while holding the Church in General Council to be infallible, were unwilling to accept the proposition that the Pope, acting alone in matters of faith and morals is infallible (cf Bishop Josip Strossmayer (1815-1905) speech at Vatican I). Many of these Catholics formed independent communities that came to be known as Old Catholic because they sought to adhere to the beliefs and practices of the Catholic Church of the post-apostolic era. These communities appealed to the Archbishop of Utrecht who consecrated the first bishops for these groups. Eventually under the leadership of the Church of Holland, the Old Catholic communities joined together to form the Utrecht Union of Churches.

The foregoing text file is a reprint of the first in a series of articles by Bishop Facione, Presiding Bishop of the Old Roman Catholic Church in North America, published originally in The Scroll by the Society of St. Mark, who has given its permission that it be freely distributed with attribution.

THE BONN AGREEMENT

The terms of the Bonn agreement (1931) which led to full communion between Old Catholics and Anglicans, and which continues to be a pattern for further intercommunion relations between the churches, reads as follows:
1. Each Communion recognizes the Catholicity and independence of the other, and maintains its own.
2. Each Communion agrees to admit members of the other Communion to participate in the Sacraments.
3. Intercommunion does not require from either Communion the acceptance of all doctrinal opinion, sacramental devotion or liturgical practice characteristic of the other, but implies that each believes the other to hold all the essentials of the Christian Faith.

WHAT DOES THIS MEAN IN PRACTICAL TERMS?

Lay people

The members of both churches may participate in each other's sacramental life and enjoy the benefits of pastoral and congregational life.

Priests

Since the orders of each church are recognized by the other, priests and deacons of Anglican and Old Catholic Churches can fully participate in each other's ministries.

Bishops

Bishops participate in the consecrations of bishops of both churches and have regular consultations at many levels.

Catechism Workbook

In your own words, answer each of the following questions, based on the information contained in the Catechism on pages 2-14.

Human Nature

Q. What are we by nature?
_____
_____

Q. What does it mean to be created in the image of God?
_____
_____
_____

Q. Why then do we live apart from God and out of harmony with creation?
_____
_____
_____

Q. Why do we not use our freedom as we should?
_____
_____
_____

Q, What help is there for us?
_____
_____

Q. How did God first help us?
_____
_____
_____

God the Father

Q. What do we learn about God as creator from the revelation to Israel?
___
___
___

Q. What does this mean?
___
___
___

Q. What does this mean about our place in the universe?
___
___
___

Q. What does this mean about human life?
___
___
___

Q. How was this revelation handed down to us?
___
___
___

The Old Covenant

Q. What is meant by a covenant with God?
___
___
___

Q. What is the Old Covenant?
_____
_____

Q. What did God promise them?
_____
_____
_____

Q. What response did God require from the chosen people?
_____
_____
_____

Q. Where is this Old Covenant to be found?
_____
_____
_____

Q. Where in the Old Testament is God's will for us shown most clearly?
_____
_____

Q. What are the Ten Commandments?
_____
_____

Q. What do we learn from these commandments?
_____
_____

Q. What is our duty to God?
_____
_____
_____

Q. What is our duty to our neighbors?

Q. What is the purpose of the Ten Commandments?

Q. Since we do not fully obey them, are they useful at all?

Sin and Redemption

Q. What is sin?

Q. How does sin have power over us?

Q. What is redemption?

Q. How did God prepare us for redemption?

Q. What is meant by the Messiah?

Q. Who do we believe is the Messiah?

God the Son

Q. What do we mean when we say that Jesus is the only Son of God?

Q. What is the nature of God revealed in Jesus?

Q. What do we mean when we say that Jesus was conceived by the power of the Holy Spirit and became incarnate from the Virgin Mary?

Q. Why did he take our human nature?

Q. What is the great importance of Jesus' suffering and death?

Q. What is the significance of Jesus' resurrection?

Q. What do we mean when we say that he descended to the dead?

Q. What do we mean when we say that he ascended into heaven and is seated at the right hand of the Father?

Q. How can we share in his victory over sin, suffering, and death?

The New Covenant

Q.   What is the New Covenant?

Q. What did the Messiah promise in the New Covenant?

Q. What response did Christ require?

Q. What are the commandments taught by Christ?

Q. What is the Summary of the Law?

Q. What is the New Commandment?

Q. Where may we find what Christians believe about Christ?

The Creeds

Q. What are the creeds?

Q. How many creeds does this Church use in its worship?

Q. What is the Apostles' Creed?

Q. What is the Nicene Creed?

Q. What, then, is the Athanasian Creed?

Q. What is the Trinity?

The Holy Spirit

Q. What is the Holy Spirit?

Q. How is the Holy Spirit revealed in the Old Covenant?

Q. How is the Holy Spirit revealed in the New Covenant?

Q. How do we recognize the presence of the Holy Spirit in our lives?

Q. How do we recognize the truths taught by the Holy Spirit?

The Holy Scriptures

Q. What are the Holy Scriptures?

Q. What is the Old Testament?

Q. What is the New Testament?

Q. What is the Apocrypha?

Q. Why do we call the Holy Scriptures the Word of God?

Q. How do we understand the meaning of the Bible?

The Church

Q. What is the Church?

Q. How is the Church described in the Bible?

Q. How is the Church described in the creeds?

Q. Why is the Church described as one?

Q. Why is the Church described as holy?

Q. Why is the Church described as catholic?

Q. Why is the Church described as apostolic?

Q. What is the mission of the Church?

Q. How does the Church pursue its mission?

Q. Through whom does the Church carry out its mission?

The Ministry

Q. Who are the ministers of the Church?

Q. What is the ministry of the laity?

Q. What is the ministry of a bishop?

Q. What is the ministry of a priest or presbyter?

Q. What is the ministry of a deacon?

Q. What is the duty of all Christians?

Prayer and Worship

Q. What is prayer?

Q. What is Christian Prayer?

Q. What prayer did Christ teach us?

Q. What are the principle kinds of prayer?

Q. What is adoration?

Q. Why do we praise God?

Q. For what do we offer thanksgiving?

Q. What is penitence?

Q. What is prayer of oblation?

Q. What are intercession and petition?

Q. What is corporate worship?

The Sacraments

Q. What are the sacraments?

Q. What is grace?

Q. What are the two great sacraments of the Gospel?

Holy Baptism

Q. What is Holy Baptism?

Q. What is the outward and visible sign in Baptism?

Q. What is the inward and spiritual grace in Baptism?

Q. What is required of us at Baptism?

Q. Why then are infants baptized?

Q. How are the promises for infants made and carried out?

The Holy Eucharist

Q. What is the Holy Eucharist?
_____
_____
_____

Q. Why is the Eucharist called a sacrifice?
_____
_____
_____

Q. By what other names is this service known?
_____
_____
_____

Q. What is the outward and visible sign in the Eucharist?
_____
_____
_____

Q. What is the inward and spiritual grace given in the Eucharist?
_____
_____
_____

Q. What are the benefits which we receive in the Lord's Supper?
_____
_____
_____

Q. What is required of us when we come to the Eucharist?
_____
_____
_____

Other Sacramental Rites

Q. What other sacramental rites evolved in the Church under the guidance of the Holy Spirit?

Q. How do they differ from the two sacraments of the Gospel?

Q. What is Confirmation?

Q. What is required of those to be confirmed?

Q. What is Ordination?

Q. What is Holy Matrimony?

Q. What is Reconciliation of a Penitent?

Q. What is Unction of the Sick?

Q. Is God's activity limited to these rites?

Q. How are the sacraments related to our Christian hope?

The Christian Hope

Q. What is the Christian hope?

Q. What do we mean by the coming of Christ in glory?

Q. What do we mean by heaven and hell?

Q. Why do we pray for the dead?

Q. What do we mean by the last judgment?
_____
_____

Q. What do we mean by the resurrection of the body?
_____
_____
_____

Q. What is the communion of saints?
_____
_____
_____

Q. What do we mean by everlasting life?
_____
_____
_____

Q. What, then, is our assurance as Christians?
_____
_____
_____

www.ingramcontent.com/pod-product-compliance
Lightning Source LLC
Chambersburg PA
CBHW020022050426
42450CB00005B/603